6
MINUTE
MORNING
CORE TRAINING

6

MINUTE
MORNING
CORE TRAINING

SARA ROSE

Bath · New York · Singapore · Hong Kong · Cologne · Delhi · Melbourne

First published by Parragon in 2009

Parragon
Queen Street House
4 Queen Street
Bath BA1 1HE, UK

ISBN: 978-1-4075-8123-1

Printed in Malaysia

Created and produced by Ivy Contract
Design: JC Lanaway
Photography: Ian Parsons
Hair and Makeup: Sarah Jane Froom and Tracy Swan
Model: Charlotte Curtis and Scott Virgo

The views expressed in this book are those of the author, but they are general views
only, and readers are urged to consult a relevant and qualified specialist for individual
advice in particular situations. Parragon hereby excludes all liability to the extent
permitted by law for any errors or omissions in this book and for any loss, damage,
or expense (whether direct or indirect) suffered by a third party relying on any
information contained in this book.

Ivy Contract would like to thank Getty Images for permission to reproduce copyright
material on pages 6 i-stock, 8 Thomas Del Brase/Stone.

Caution
Please check with your doctor/therapist before attempting this workout, particularly
if you have an injury, are pregnant, or have just had a baby. It is recommended that
new mothers wait at least six weeks postpartum before participating in exercise (12
weeks if it was a Cesarean birth). If you feel any pain or discomfort at any point,
please stop exercising immediately and seek medical advice.

CONTENTS

INTRODUCTION

Core training is a workout that strengthens your body from the inside out by concentrating on the muscles that form your "core." The core of your body is simply what's between the shoulders and hips—basically, the trunk and pelvis. Draw an imaginary line around the center of your body, starting at your navel; most of the muscles bordering that line are your core muscles. Core training reeducates these muscles to make them more effective.

The core is a crucial group of muscles, not only for sports, but for normal daily activities as well because it comes into play just about every time you move. The core acts to produce force (for example, during lifting), it stabilizes the body to permit other musculature to produce force (for example, during running), and it's also called upon to transfer energy (for example, during jumping). This is why it is so important that your core is strong. Once you have learned how to strengthen your core, your lower abdominal muscles will be drawn in toward the spine and help you sit up straight. Your balance and coordination will be improved and, most important of all, the stability these muscles bring will help keep your spine healthy and flexible.

How to use this book

The exercises in this book are designed to fit into 6-minute sessions, so you should be able to find the time to squeeze a workout into even your busiest day. Exercises are grouped into suggested programs at the end of the book, but you can mix and match the routines to suit your requirements.

What is core stability?

Core stability is the effective use of the core muscles to help stabilize the spine, allowing your limbs to move more freely. Good core stability means you can keep your midsection rigid without forces such as gravity affecting your movements. The positive effects of this include reducing the chance of injury, better posture, increased agility and flexibility, and improved coordination.

Core stability can be increased by developing trunk fitness, which is necessary for everyday life, not just for sports. To pick up a child, for example, requires a core strength not only to lift the child but also to do it in a safe way that avoids injury. To really capture the benefits of core strength, including better alignment, balance, and functional movement (as well as flat abdominal muscles), it is necessary to work the deep abdominal and back musculature.

How to train your core

Traditional abdominal training is not the ideal way to train your core. Endless crunches are not only monotonous, but also ineffective because they do not target the deep muscles. The abdominals are muscles just like any other and should be trained using the same principles as any other muscle group. This means they should be loaded with resistance and challenged in a variety of ways—by lateral (side) flexion, bending forward and backward, and rotation. If strength and muscle development are the goals, hundreds of repetitions are not necessary. Core strength should be developed gradually to avoid the risk of injury. When starting out on a core training program, you need to progress properly:

- Start with the easiest movement, then move on to the more difficult ones.
- You may not require any extra load to start with but, as you adapt, you can increase the resistance by using weights, changing the position, etc.
- Perform all movements in a slow and controlled manner until your coordination, strength, and confidence allow higher-speed movements.
- To increase the complexity and muscle demands of the exercises, many moves can be performed lying prone (facedown) or supine (on your back) on an unstable platform after you have mastered them on the floor. Using an exercise ball or a wobble board (see page 13) may be difficult for beginners, so progress to this stage when you are ready.

All about the spine

The spine is an S shaped flexible curve that supports your skull, acts as a structural base for your limbs, ribs, and pelvis to attach to, and enables you to stand upright. It also provides movement for your trunk, allowing you to bend forward, backward, side to side, and twist.

The spine has three natural curves: in at the back of the neck, outward at the back of the rib cage, and in again at the lower back (lumbar spine). To protect your spine, you should aim to maintain its natural curve, particularly in the lumbar region. This is called putting your spine into "neutral," and nearly every exercise in this book will require you to do this. It's essential that you can perform this maneuver correctly, so use the following instructions as a guide:

Standing Neutral

1 Stand tall against a wall with your buttocks and shoulders touching the wall. Keep your feet parallel and hips' width apart, with your weight evenly distributed on both feet. Gently pull up through your legs, keeping your knees slightly bent, and pull your tailbone down toward the floor.

Standing

Learning how to stand in neutral is important to minimize the stress on ligaments and disks.

2 Place your hand between the wall and your lower back. The neutral position is slightly different for everyone, but it should feel comfortable and you should just be able to place the flat of your hand between your back and the wall. If only your fingers can get through, your back is too flat and your pelvis is tilted too far forward. If you can get your whole hand through, then your back is too arched and your pelvis too far back.

2

Lying Down Neutral

1 Lie down on your back, with your knees bent and your feet flat on the floor, hips' width apart. Your spine will be flat against the floor, apart from the curve of the neck and the lower back.

2 Press your waist back onto the floor by tilting your pelvis back so that you lose the curve in your lower back. Now tilt your pelvis forward so that your lower back overarches. Then find the midpoint between these two extremes. You should be able to slip one hand under your waist and feel a slight gap between your waist and the floor.

Sitting Neutral

1 Sit up straight on a stool, chair, or exercise ball, with your weight evenly distributed on both buttocks. Keep your feet flat on the floor, hips' width apart.

2 Look straight ahead, and keep your spine and neck long. Pull your shoulder blades down toward the waist to stop your shoulders from hunching.

3 The natural curves at your neck and waist should be evident.

2

Protecting your spine while exercising

• Be conscious of your neck—it's fine to cradle the sides of your head with your hands, but avoid resting your head on your hands because you may pull on your neck.
• Keep your abdominal muscles pulled in—this will protect your lower spine.
• Exercise on a mat or other padded surface to prevent bruising.
• Always keep your knees slightly bent when performing leg exercises—straight-leg exercising makes your hip flexors pull directly on the spine, causing excessive stress on your lower back.

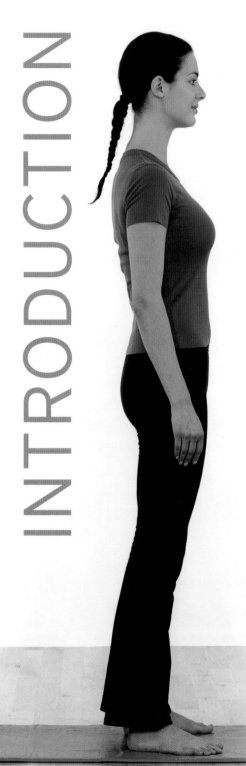

INTRODUCTION

Posture

The alignment of your muscles and joints is known as "posture." If your posture is consistently poor over a period of time, your muscles will be subjected to uneven stresses, leading to aching muscles and joints, tiredness, weakness, and an increased risk of injury when exercising.

Good posture looks natural and relaxed, not slouched and hunched. When you are standing up, your neck should be in line with your spine, with your head balanced squarely on top, your shoulder blades set back and down, and your spine long and curving naturally. Your hips should be straight. Good posture when sitting means sitting up straight with your feet flat on the floor and your lower back supported.

How to check your posture

Stand sideways in front of a full-length mirror to assess your posture. Imagine there is a straight line drawn down the center of your body. If your posture is correct, the line will pass through the center of the earlobe, the tip of the shoulder, halfway through the chest, slightly behind the hip, and just outside the ankle bone.

It does take time to correct any postural deficiencies you may have, but it is important to identify what your weaknesses are—for example, rounded shoulders—so that you can work on correcting these. The good news is that, by training your core muscles, you will be strengthening the muscles that hold up your back and automatically improving your posture.

Tips for improving posture

• Sleep on your back rather than on your front.
• Keep your head up and your shoulders back when walking.
• Bend your knees rather than your back when bending over to pick something up.
• Brace your abdominal muscles before lifting heavy objects; bend your knees rather than your back to pick it up, then carry it close to your body.
• If you tend to carry a lot in your shoulder bag or briefcase, you would be better off using a backpack to disperse the weight evenly.

Core muscles

The muscles you need to know about for improving your core stability are those that are arranged around your torso.

Abdominal muscles

The abdominal muscles support the spine, protect internal organs, and enable you to sit, twist, and bend. The rectus abdominis is the muscle that runs from the bottom of your ribs to the pubic bone. It creates the "six-pack" look, but its actual purpose is to let you bend forward and sit up from a lying position. At the side of the torso are two diagonal muscles: the internal oblique and the external oblique. These bend the spine to the side and rotate it. Underneath the obliques lies the transversus abdominis, the deepest layer of muscles in your core, which wraps horizontally around your torso like a corset from the rib cage to the pubic bone, until it merges with the sheath over the rectus abdominis. The transversus abdominis is responsible for trunk stability and pulls your abdomen in tight.

Back muscles

There are two groups of back muscles that are important to core stability. The first group attaches between each of the vertebrae; the second along the whole length of the spine. The multifidus is the most important of these because it stiffens the spine and can also flatten the lumbar curve without moving the whole spine.

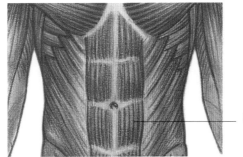
Rectus abdominis

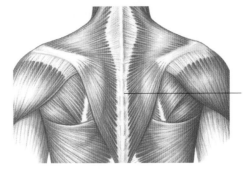
Multifidus

Pubococcygeus muscles

These attach to the inside of the pelvis, forming a sling from the tailbone, at the back to the pubic bone at the front. The pubococcygeus muscles are vital for continence and help to maintain intra-abdominal pressure, which is key to stablization.

Trunk muscles

The trunk muscles fall into two categories: inner (mainly responsible for stabilization) and outer (mainly responsible for movement). The inner-unit muscles include the transversus abdominis, diaphragm, multifidus, and pelvic floor; the outer unit includes the obliques and spinal erectors. The inner and outer units work together to create spinal stability and enable subsequent movement.

Before you start core training, it is a good idea to become familiar with your abdominal muscles and to get used to breathing correctly. You may also find some extra equipment will be useful.

Setting your abdominal muscles

This means tightening the transversus abdominis so that it maintains stability of the spine while you are exercising. It is also known as abdominal "hollowing," "setting," or "bracing." Doing this correctly is vital for successful core training.

Standing abdominal hollowing

1 Stand upright with your feet hips' width apart. Keep your spine in neutral.

2 Focus on your navel and draw it in by tightening your muscles, not by sucking in your waist or holding your breath. Restrict the movement to your abdominal muscles; do not tilt your pelvis or flatten your back.

Kneeling abdominal hollowing

1 Position yourself on all fours (the "box" position), with your hands and knees shoulders' width apart.

2 Let your abdominal muscles relax and sag downward, then tighten them and pull them up and in. The amount of movement may be very small to begin with but should increase to about 4 inches (10 cm) with practice. Don not arch your back or tilt your pelvis—the movement should be restricted to the abdominal area.

Prone abdominal hollowing

1 Lie facedown on the floor with your arms by your sides, palms up. Place a cushion beneath your forehead for comfort.

2 Pull your navel up and inward and draw your abdominal wall off the floor, but do not lift your chest. If you have excess weight on your abdomen, you may not be able to do this.

Sitting abdominal hollowing

1 Sit on a stool or exercise ball with your feet apart.

2 Sit up straight and place one hand on your abdomen and the other in the small of your back—this will help you to monitor the position of your spine. Pull your navel in and up, away from your front hand.

2

Prone abdominal hollowing

Equipment and preparation

A little preparation goes a long way when it comes to exercising. The amount of equipment you need is up to you—there are plenty of pieces of equipment that create an unstable base and make your core muscles work really hard. These range from wobble boards to medicine balls, exercise balls, resistance bands, and even adjustable cable pulley machines if you are in the gym. For the purposes of this book, we recommend an exercise ball and/or a wobble board for variation. Hand weights and ankle weights can be used (but not if you are new to exercise or have back problems)—make sure they are not too heavy. Small cushions or folded towels make ideal padding during exercises that involve lying on the floor or kneeling.

Find a quiet, comfortable, clutter-free space to work out in. You need a nonslip surface, such as an exercise mat or a carpet, to protect your spine and prevent bruising. If possible, try to exercise in front of a full-length mirror so that you can check what you are doing.

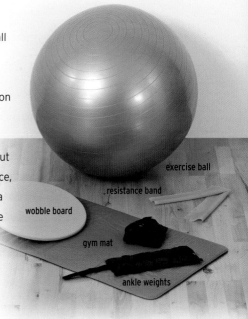

exercise ball

resistance band

wobble board

gym mat

ankle weights

Breathing

Breathing is something we all do without thinking, but it can be consciously controlled. Correct breathing comes from the deepest area of the lungs, but most of us have shallow, rapid breathing and use only the top third of the lungs. Breathing properly encourages effective oxygenation of the blood, allowing muscles and organs to work efficiently. It also relaxes muscles, releases tension, and enables you to contract your inner core properly. You need to practice abdominal, or diaphragmatic, breathing, which allows the lungs to fill and empty with minimal effort. This will make your exercising much more effective—though you will find it very difficult to do at first.

1 Sit in a comfortable position with your back supported. Place one hand on your chest and the other on your abdomen just below the breastbone. If the hand on your chest moves more than the one on your abdomen as you breathe, then your breathing is mainly in the upper chest. Try to breathe so that only your lower hand is moving.

2 Now place both hands on your abdomen just below the ribs. Breathe in slowly through your nose. Pause for a few seconds, then breathe out through your mouth, letting out as much air as possible and feeling your abdomen fall as your diaphragm relaxes. Repeat 3 or 4 times.

It is important to warm up the specific muscles and joints that you will be using in order to prevent injury. A warm-up should replicate the movements you are about to do, but should graduate in intensity and range to mobilize the relevant body parts in all directions.

Standing Pelvic Tilt

Pelvic tilting teaches you how to control the lumbar spine during exercise. The aim is to practice finding your neutral spine position. The action should be confined to your lower back–avoiding any body sway.

2

1 Stand tall against a wall with your feet hips' width apart, arms by your sides.

2 Tilt your hips back and forth a few times. When tilting your pelvis forward, you should be able to fit your hand into the gap between your lower back and the wall as your lower back hollows. When tilting your pelvis backward you should feel your lower back press against your hand as it flattens. Aim to find the midpoint of this spinal movement, between the two extremes–this is your neutral spine position.

Standing Abdominal Hollowing

For all the core stability exercises, you have to activate the deep inner-unit muscles in a hollowing action; therefore, the abdominal hollowing exercise that rehearses this action is essential as part of your warm-up. The action itself should feel light and subtle–do not hold your breath or suck in your waist and keep your hips, legs, and spine still (see page 12).

2

1 Stand tall with your feet hips' width apart and your spine in neutral.

2 Pull your abdomen in and up to hollow your abdomen, keeping your attention focused on your navel. Imagine that there is a belt around your waist and that you are simply tightening the belt one notch. Hold for a count of 5. Perform 3 repetitions.

2

2

Torso Rotations

Gradually increase the range of movement as you do this exercise, reaching across your torso with your opposite hand as you do so. The twisting action should force you to come up onto the toes of your opposite foot.

1 Keep your pelvis in neutral and stand with your feet hips' width apart and knees slightly bent.

2 Rotate your torso to one side, then the other, increasing the range of movement as you do so. You should feel a slight stretch across your back and shoulders. Perform 5-10 repetitions.

Spinal Curl

This exercise will create flexibility and strength in your spine and relax your shoulders.

1 Stand with your feet hips' width apart and your knees slightly bent. Bend your knees and put your hands on your thighs, just above the knees.

2 Push your buttocks away and let your lower spine curl downward, making a concave shape.

3 Now, tightening your abdominal muscles, arch your lower back upward, then release back to the concave shape.

4 Perform 5-10 repetitions, increasing the movement with each repetition.

BE AWARE

Always check with your doctor before embarking on an exercise routine— this is essential if you have ever had any back problems.

In this section you will find basic standing and sitting exercises to improve core stability. Many are traditional abdominal exercises or established moves from exercise systems such as yoga and Pilates and have varying degrees of difficulty.

Roll Down the Wall

This is a great warm-up exercise for your back. The aim is to lengthen the spine and increase its flexibility, strengthen your abdominal muscles, and help build core strength. Keep your breathing controlled and regular throughout.

1 Stand about 1 foot (30 cm) away from a wall with your feet parallel, hips' width apart and your knees slightly bent. Lean back on the wall to support your spine. Put your pelvis in neutral and tighten your abdominal muscles.

2 Slowly roll down off the wall by dropping your chin toward your chest, and then letting the weight of your head draw you downward, trying to avoid swaying from side to side. Let your arms dangle down.

3 Roll down as far as is comfortable (ideally, until your hands touch the floor), then reverse the motion so that you come back up to a standing position. Perform 5 repetitions.

Standing Forward Bend

This stretches and strengthens your spine, helps you to stand properly, and helps build core strength.

1 Stand up straight with your spine in neutral and your feet close together, knees slightly bent, and your arms by your sides. Set your abdominal muscles.

2 Bend forward until your body is at a 90-degree angle and your hands are behind you. Return to the starting position. Perform 5 repetitions.

2

Horizontal Balance

The aim in this exercise is to keep your balance with minimal movement—avoid tilting your pelvis as you bend forward.

1 Stand up straight with your knees slightly bent and your spine in neutral. Tighten your abdominal muscles.

2 Transfer your weight onto one leg and bend at the hip so that you lean forward, extending the other leg behind you as you bend and extending your arms forward.

3 Lean forward as far as possible or until you are horizontal. Hold for a count of 5, then return to the starting position. Repeat on the other leg.

Tai chi

There are many forms of exercise and movement therapies that will help to improve core stability. Tai chi, a noncombative martial art, is very useful for core training because of its emphasis on balance and good posture.

2

3

2

3 Hold for a count of 3, then release. Repeat with the other leg. Perform 4-6 repetitions.

3

Standing Leg Lift

This will help improve your balance, stabilize the pelvis, and tone your thigh and hip muscles. Aim to keep your pelvis stable throughout.

1 Stand with your spine in neutral, feet slightly apart, and arms by your sides.

2 Pull your navel in toward your spine and bring your left knee in toward your chest so that your big toe is resting on the side of your right knee. Hold your knee with both hands, keeping your spine straight and your standing leg strong. You will need to drop your left hip down and lift the hip higher on the right side to keep your hips level at this point.

Variation

To make this exercise more difficult, after step 2 stretch your left leg straight out in front of you at hip height, holding onto the back of your thigh to support it. Release your arms and rest them on your buttocks, but keep your left leg extended in front of you. Hold for up to 10 seconds, then lower your leg to the floor and repeat on the other leg. Perform 4-6 repetitions on each leg.

2

Side Standing Leg Lift

This works your abdominal muscles and back extensors, as well as your quadriceps, hamstrings, and gluteals (buttock muscles).

1 Stand up straight with your spine in neutral, your feet hips' width apart, and your arms by your sides. Set your abdominal muscles.

2 Support your body weight on your right leg and lift your left leg to the side. As you do this, extend your right arm forward and your left arm out to the side. Hold for a count of 3.

3 Repeat on the other side. Perform 6-8 repetitions.

Lunge

The farther you step forward in this exercise, the harder your muscles will be worked.

1 Stand with your hands on your hips and your feet parallel and hips' width apart. Set your abdominal muscles.

2 Take a big step forward, keeping your weight evenly distributed between both legs.

3 Bend both knees as far as is comfortable so that you lower your torso down, then return to the starting position.

4 Repeat on the other leg. Perform 6-8 repetitions.

BE AWARE
Add ankle weights for an increased challenge, but only when you can perform the leg lifts perfectly.

3

Basic Squat

Keep your spine in neutral and do not allow your pelvis to tilt as you squat down.

1 Start by standing in a level position, with your feet parallel and hips' width apart, and your hands on your hips. Keep your spine in neutral alignment and tighten your abdominal muscles. Bend your knees as if you are about to sit down.

2 Squat down as far as you can manage without losing your balance or arching your back.

3 Hold for a count of 1, then push through your heels to return to the starting position. Perform 6-8 repetitions.

Squat with Leg Lift

This move works your entire lower body. Focus on keeping your abdominal muscles braced to maintain your balance.

1 Stand on the floor with your feet parallel and hips' width apart. Place your hands on your hips, set your abdominal muscles, and bend your knees so that you squat back.

2 Press up into a standing position as you simultaneously extend your right leg to the side.

3 Return to the squatting position. Repeat on the other side. Perform 6-8 repetitions.

2

Sitting Forward Spine Stretch

This exercise helps you to sit with good posture because it strengthens your transversus abdominis. Make sure you do not hunch your shoulders.

Sitting Spinal Twist

This exercise works your obliques. Aim to keep your spine straight without rounding your back.

1 Sit on the floor with your legs extended in front of you, knees slightly bent, and feet flexed. Set your abdominal muscles and extend your arms in front of you at chest level.

2 Curl your body forward, keeping your abdominal muscles pulled back in toward your spine.

3 Roll back to the starting position, using your abdominal muscles to pull yourself up. Perform 4 repetitions.

BE AWARE
Remember—it's the quality of movement that counts, rather than the number of repetitions.

1 Sit up straight with your legs extended in front of you, knees slightly bent and feet flexed. Raise your arms to the sides at shoulder height and tighten your abdominal muscles to support your back.

2 Turn your head and shoulders toward your left, keeping your back, hips, and buttocks motionless as you move.

3 Rotate as far as is comfortable, then hold for a count of 1. Return to the starting position and repeat the exercise on the other side.

4 Perform 6-8 repetitions on each side, rotating a little farther the easier the movement becomes.

Variation
Sit on an exercise ball while doing spinal twists to further challenge your core muscles. Keep your knees still during this exercise—if they do move, this shows that your pelvis is not stable.

Sitting Leg Lift

Sitting on an exercise ball and lifting your feet from the floor is a great way to train your core muscles. This exercise challenges your balance and helps you control movement of the pelvis. It's important to use your core muscles to keep your pelvis stable throughout the exercise.

1 Sit up straight on an exercise ball with your spine in neutral. Raise your arms out to your sides at shoulder height to help you balance and tighten your abdominal muscles to support your lower back. Your feet should be on the floor, parallel, and hips' width apart.

2 Keeping your knee bent, lift your right leg about 4 inches (10 cm) off the floor, and hold for a count of 10, making sure you do not arch your back as you do so. Do not lift your feet too high or you will wobble and lose your postural alignment.

3 Repeat on the left leg. Perform 3-5 repetitions.

BE AWARE
To make the exercise harder, lift both feet off the floor at the same time.

2

Sitting Pelvic Tilt

Try to keep your upper body relatively still as you perform this exercise. You can increase the size of the movements to make your abdominal muscles work even harder to maintain your balance.

1 Sit with good posture on an exercise ball with your spine in neutral and your feet shoulders' width apart. Keep your arms down by your sides or fold in front of you at shoulder height.

2 Set your abdominal muscles by gently pulling your navel in toward your spine.

3 Gently tilt your pelvis backward and forward using very small movements, so that you are slightly increasing the curve in your back then flattening it. Perform 10-15 repetitions.

3

Mermaid

This exercise works your obliques and increases lateral flexion. Try to keep your spine straight and do not lean forward or backward. If you do not have an exercise ball, you can kneel with your feet under your buttocks instead.

1 Sit up on the ball with good posture, your spine in neutral, and your feet parallel on the floor and hips' width apart. Tighten your abdominal muscles and let your arms simply rest by your sides.

2 Reach your right arm up to the ceiling and lean over to the left side so that your right arm reaches over your head. Hold for a count of 1, then lower your arm.

3 Repeat on the other side. Perform 3 repetitions.

2

Alexander Technique

This is a method that aims to improve posture so that your body operates with minimum strain. Students relearn basic movements, such as sitting and standing, and how to align the body so they can move in a relaxed, fluid way.

Sitting Reverse Abdominal Curl

This is an easy exercise that can be done almost anywhere. It works your rectus abdominis. Try to avoid sagging or arching the back and hold in your abdominal muscles tightly throughout the movement.

1 Sit on a stool or bench with your spine in neutral. Set your abdominal muscles and extend your arms in front of you at shoulder height.

2 Slowly lean your torso and shoulders backward, keeping the spine rigid, as far back as is comfortable.

3 Hold the position for a count of 2 then return to the starting position. Perform 6-8 repetitions.

Sitting Lateral Curl

This is a challenging exercise and should be attempted only when you are confident that you can easily maintain your balance on an exercise ball. It gives all your abdominal muscles a good workout. To increase the stabilization control required, bring your feet closer together at the start.

1 Sit on the ball, with your spine in neutral and your feet hips' width apart. Set your abdominal muscles and roll forward with your pelvis until the ball is under your lower spine.

2 Put your hands on either side of your head.

3 Lift your upper torso toward your knees and over to the right side. At the same time, lift your right leg toward your left shoulder, bending the knee.

4 Hold for a count of 3, then release slowly and return to the starting position. Repeat on the other side. Perform 6-8 repetitions.

This section has a range of floor exercises designed to improve core stability and develop strength and flexibility. Don't worry if you can't complete the full range of movement suggested in each exercise—as you become more in shape this will become easier.

Backstroke

This exercise helps you practice keeping your torso still while the arms move. It also helps to strengthen the lumbar spine.

1 Lie on your back with a pillow under your head and your arms at your sides. Keep your pelvis in neutral and tighten your abdominal muscles.

2 Lift up your left arm to the sky and sweep it back toward the floor behind you, without actually touching the floor. Bring your left arm back up to the center, then bring your right arm up to the same point, so that both your arms are straight above your chest, shoulders' width apart.

3 Take your right arm backward and your left arm forward, then bring your right arm back to the center, followed by your left arm. Perform 6-8 repetitions, then repeat starting with the other arm.

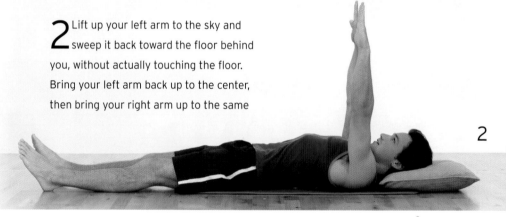

BE AWARE
Keep your arms wide during this exercise—they should not brush your ears. Keep your body in alignment and the back of the rib cage in contact with the floor throughout.

2

3

Dog

This classic yoga position strengthens and stretches most of your body. As your flexibility increases, you will be able to press your heels into the floor.

1 Start on all fours with your hands under your shoulders and your knees under your hips, hips-width apart. Keep your spine in neutral and slowly tighten your abdominal muscles.

2 Try to curl your toes under, press back into your palms, and, bringing the balls of your feet onto the floor, lift your hips toward the ceiling and straighten your legs until you are forming an inverted V shape.

3 Hold briefly, then come down again on all fours. Perform 4 repetitions.

Rolling Like a Ball

This exercise improves your balance and the flexibility of your spine, and builds strong abdominal muscles.

1 Sit up with your knees bent and hold your knees with your hands. Pull your abdominal muscles toward your spine to help keep your balance. Tuck your chin into your chest and, staying balanced on your tailbone, lift both feet off the floor.

2 Roll back slowly, bringing your knees closer to your nose until your shoulder blades touch the floor, making sure you do not roll back onto your neck. Then roll forward to the starting position. Perform 3-5 repetitions.

Pilates

This body-conditioning technique focuses on strengthening the core postural muscles to increase your flexibility and mobility.

FLOOR EXERCISES

Basic Curl on an Exercise Ball

This strengthens your rectus abdominis as well as increasing the flexibility of your spine. To make this exercise harder, cross your hands over your chest or behind your head, and bring your feet closer together.

1 Lie on an exercise ball so that your lumbar and midspine are supported by the ball. Keep your feet wide apart for stability and your knees bent. Keep your arms by your sides so that your hands are either side of your buttocks.

BE AWARE

Keep your movements slow and controlled, and do not lift too much—it's the quality of movement that counts.

2 Contract your abdominal muscles and curl upward and forward, slowly curling your rib cage toward your pelvis and stretching your arms out in front of you for balance.

3 Hold briefly, then slowly release and return to the starting position. Perform 6-8 repetitions.

1

2

Reverse Curl

This works your lower abdominal muscles. You will find that your knees naturally move toward your chest in this exercise, but concentrate on lifting your hips, rather than swinging your legs.

1 Lie on your back on the floor with your legs raised, knees bent over your hips, and ankles crossed. Keep your arms by your sides, palms facing down.

2 Tighten your abdominal muscles, pulling your navel down toward your spine. Slowly bring your knees toward your chest, then lower them by gently tilting your pelvis. Perform 6-8 repetitions.

Oblique Curl

This exercise works your obliques. Try not to pull on your head.

1 Lie flat on your back, with your knees bent and feet flat on the floor, hips' width apart.

2 Cross your left ankle over your right knee. Place your right hand behind your head, elbow bent, and put your left hand on the floor for support.

3 Brace your abdominal muscles and slowly curl up and over, bringing your right arm toward your left knee, then slowly lower to the starting position. Perform 6-8 repetitions, then repeat on the other side.

Basic Bridge

Bridges and planks are static exercises that enable you to assess your core strength by the length of time you are able to hold the positions. However, they are only effective if you maintain a flat line from your shoulders to your feet.

1 Lie on your back with your knees bent, feet parallel and hips' width apart, and the heels close to your buttocks. Keep your arms close by your sides.

2 Tighten your abdominal muscles and tilt your pelvis as you would do in a pelvic tilt.

3 Press your feet down firmly and gently lift your hips, lower back and mid back off the floor. Aim to align your hips with your thighs and body. Hold for a count of 10, then release and lower slowly to the floor. Relax. Perform 2 repetitions.

Variation

Bridging using an exercise ball makes your rectus abdominis and external obliques work harder. Lie on your back with your arms by your sides. Place your legs on the ball so that it is resting under your calf muscles. Tighten your abdominal muscles and lift your hips off the floor until your body is in a diagonal line from shoulders to knees. Hold for a count of 10–15, then release and lower slowly to the floor. Relax, then perform 2 repetitions.

Variation

BE AWARE
Use your hands for balance, but do not push yourself up.

3

Bridge with Leg Extension

Lifting one leg from an exercise ball will strengthen the muscles at the back of your buttocks and thighs, while increasing balance and control in the stabilizing muscle groups. Do not let your back arch and keep the ball as still as possible throughout.

1 Lie on your back with your arms outstretched. Place your legs on the ball so that it is resting under your calves. Gently tighten your abdominal muscles.

2 Lift up your hips until your body is diagonal from shoulders to knees.

3 With your foot flexed, slowly raise one leg about 1 foot (30 cm) off the ball and hold for a count of 10. Slowly release. Repeat using the other leg. Perform 6-8 repetitions.

1

2

Feldenkrais method

This is a system of physical reeducation designed to improve posture and movement. Simple exercises increase body awareness and mobility, and are said to improve both mental and physical health.

3

FLOOR EXERCISES

Reverse Bridge on an Exercise Ball

This exercise improves your balance while working your abdominal muscles, lower back, pelvic stabilizers, gluteals, and hamstring muscles. Here, you roll into position and roll out again. To increase the difficulty of this exercise you can raise and lower alternate legs once you are in position. The aim is to keep your spine in neutral throughout—do not lift your hips too high.

1 Sit on the ball with your hands by your sides and feet flat on the floor, hips' width apart.

2 Walk your feet forward, rolling your hips down and lying back on the ball as you do so. Stop when your shoulder blades are on the ball.

3 Lower your head to the ball and lift your hips so that your torso is in a straight line, tightening your abdominal muscles as you do so. Hold for a count of 10.

4 Slowly drop your hips and lift your head off the ball.

5 Walk your feet back, pressing your lower back into the ball as you go, and return to the starting position. Perform 2 repetitions.

3

4

Plank

This exercise works your entire abdominal area as well as your lower back. Use your abdominal muscles to keep your torso stable and not tipped to one side.

1 Lie facedown on the floor with your elbows under your shoulders and your forearms on the floor.

2 Keep your spine in neutral and tighten your abdominal muscles.

3 Lift your legs and torso away from the floor, keeping your weight supported through your shoulders, forearms, and curled toes.

4 Hold the position for 15-20 seconds, until you begin to lose abdominal tension. Relax and rest for 10 seconds. Perform 3 repetitions.

BE AWARE
To make this exercise easier, perform the movement with your knees on the floor instead of going up onto your toes.

Push-up on a Wobble Board

Try to keep the board stable throughout. You can also use an exercise ball or any other suitable unstable base for this exercise. To increase the difficulty, raise alternate legs with each push-up.

1 Hold on to the edges of the board, facedown, with your legs extended behind you, hips' width apart, and your toes curled under.

2 Keep your spine in neutral and tighten your abdominal muscles.

3 Slowly bend your elbows and lower your chest toward the board.

4 Hold briefly, then push yourself back up into the starting position. Perform 6-8 repetitions.

BE AWARE
This exercise can be challenging. To make it a little easier, just raise your hips and torso away from the floor in step 3 so that your weight is supported by your knees and not your toes.

Swan

This lengthens and strengthens your spine, as well as works your abdominal muscles. To maintain the tension in your abdominals during this exercise, imagine that you are trying to lift your abdomen off the ground.

1 Lie facedown with your arms extended in front of you and your legs extended behind you.

2 Keep your spine in neutral and tighten your abdominal muscles. You should feel your pubic bone pressing down into the floor.

3 Raise your shoulders and feet a few inches off the ground, hold for a count of 10, then release. Perform 2 repetitions.

2

3

Variation

Performing this move on an exercise ball strengthens and stretches your back. Do not attempt this exercise if you can feel any discomfort in your lower back; stop immediately. Lie with the ball under your stomach and pelvis. Plant your curled toes on the floor, hips' width apart, and keep your legs straight. Place your hands on the floor, shoulders' width apart. Tighten your abdominal muscles and lift your head so that there is a long line from your head to your heels. Slowly push your pelvis into the ball as you look up and extend your spine away from the ball. Hold for a count of 5, then release. Perform 3 repetitions.

BE AWARE

Consult a doctor before doing this exercise if you have ever had any lower-back problems.

Variation

Supine Leg Lift

The importance of this exercise is to hold the legs off the floor with correct spinal alignment and abdominal bracing. Use small ankle weights for extra challenge.

1 Lie on your back with your knees bent and feet on the floor, hips' width apart.

2 Keep your spine and pelvis in neutral and gently tighten your abdominal muscles.

3 Keeping your knees bent, slowly lift your right leg about 6-8 inches (15-20 cm) off the floor and hold in position.

4 Now lift your left leg off the floor and bring it up next to the right leg.

5 Slowly lower your right leg back to the floor, then the left leg. Perform 6-8 repetitions.

BE AWARE
Each leg movement should be slow and controlled.

Prone Leg Raise

Leg raises stretch and strengthen your abdominal muscles, lengthen your lower spine, and strengthen your lower back. Keep your hip bones down on the floor as you do this exercise.

1 Lie facedown on the floor with your arms folded in front of you and your head resting on top of your arms.

2 Keep your pelvis in neutral and gently tighten your abdominal muscles so that your pubic bone is pressing down into the floor. Keep your buttock muscles tight, too.

3 Lift one leg about 6 inches (15 cm) off the floor. Hold for a count of 5, then release and raise the other leg. Perform 3-5 repetitions.

3

Scissors

You will feel a stretch in your hamstrings as you perform this exercise, but the main aims are to keep your pelvis, hips, and spine still and maintain abdominal tension throughout.

1 Lie on your back with both legs raised, toes pointing toward the ceiling and knees slightly bent.

2 Keep your spine in neutral and set your abdominal muscles.

3 Slowly lower your left leg down toward the floor, still keeping your torso in alignment. From this position, change the position of your legs in a scissoring action. Perform 6-8 repetitions on each leg.

3

Supine Back Extension

This lengthens and strengthens your back, as well as working on your core muscles.

1 Lie with your middle and lower back on an exercise ball, with your knees bent and your feet hips' width apart and flat on the floor. Put your hands by the sides of your head for support.

2 Pull your navel in toward your spine to set your abdominal muscles. Let your spine arch backward and relax over the ball and rock gently to and fro for a count of 10. Perform 2 repetitions.

3 To get out of this position safely, drop your pelvis to the floor and roll off the ball.

1

2

FLOOR EXERCISES

Superman

This strengthens your back and abdominal muscles and lengthens your spine. Avoid arching your back and aim to keep your movements slow so that you maintain your balance.

1 Position yourself on the floor on all fours. Keep your spine in neutral and set your abdominal muscles.

2 Raise your left arm and your right leg off the floor. Hold this position for up to 10 seconds before returning to the starting position.

3 Repeat with the opposite arm and leg. Perform 6-8 repetitions.

Variation

You can do this exercise over an exercise ball, but you need to be adept at balancing on the ball. Lie facedown over an exercise ball so that your fingers and toes are touching the floor. Raise your left arm and your right leg off the floor at the same time.

1

2

Single-Leg Stretch

This exercise will help you learn to stabilize your abdominal muscles and hips, and will work your entire abdominal area. It will also stretch your back and legs.

BE AWARE
Try to extend your straight leg as much as possible.

1 Lie on your back with your pelvis in neutral. Bend your knees and rest your feet on an exercise ball. Keep your arms by your sides and rest your head on a flat pillow.

2 Set your abdominal muscles and raise your right leg into the air up toward the ceiling, pressing your left leg into the ball.

3 Bring down your right leg and repeat on the left leg. Perform 6–8 repetitions.

Double-Leg Stretch

This exercise will make your deep stabilizing muscles work to control the weight and movement of your legs. Along with strengthening your deep abdominal muscles and inner thigh muscles, this exercise aims to build a strong center that remains stable when you move your arms and legs.

1 Lie on your back with your knees bent and your arms by your sides.

2 Keep your spine in neutral and tighten your abdominal muscles. Pick up the exercise ball between your ankles and squeeze together, pulling your knees toward you.

3 Gently sit up far enough that you are resting your upper body on your elbows.

4 Straighten out your legs diagonally and hold for a count of 5. Return to the starting position. Perform 6–8 repetitions.

Side Leg Circles

This exercise tones and strengthens your core muscles, as well as the hips, buttocks, and inner thighs.

1 Lie on your right side with your head supported by your right hand and your right arm supported by a cushion or pillow. Rest your left hand on the floor in front of you.

2 Bend your right leg in front of you for support.

3 Keep your spine in neutral and set your abdominal muscles.

4 Point your left foot and raise your left leg, raising it as high as feels comfortable. Then draw 5 small clockwise circles with your toes, keeping your abdominal muscles strong throughout and moving from your hip joint.

5 Reverse the direction and draw 5 small counterclockwise circles, then slowly release. Perform 6-8 repetitions, then repeat on the other side.

BE AWARE
Keep your torso in line throughout and don't let it sink forward.

COOLING DOWN

It is essential to stretch after any exercise routine to release the tension in your muscles and reduce any stiffness or tightness in the joints. These should be done only when the muscles are warm. Keep your abdominal muscles braced to protect your lower back.

Sitting Spinal Stretch

This movement stretches and rotates your abdomen, ribs, and spine, and stretches your hip muscles. Make sure you move from your hips up, not from your shoulders down.

1 Sit up straight with your legs out in front of you.

2 Bend your right knee and pull your right foot into your left buttock. Bend your left knee and place your left foot on your right knee.

3 Gently draw in your navel toward your spine to set your abdominal muscles and slowly rotate to the left. Use your left hand to help keep your body upright. Rotate as far as is comfortable and hold the stretch for at least a count of 15.

4 Release and return to the starting position, then rearrange your legs so that your right one is on top. Rotate to the other side of your body.

1

3

BE AWARE
Aim to keep your spine straight throughout and do not arch your back.

Knee Hug

This will stretch and release the muscles in your lower back.

1 Lie on your back with your legs in the air and your knees bent. Tighten your abdominal muscles to protect your lower back.

2 Lift your knees to your chest and hold onto your shins.

3 Pull your knees in as tightly as is comfortable and hold for at least 15 seconds. Slowly release, return to the starting position, and repeat.

Child's Pose

This classic yoga position is great for relaxing your entire back.

1 Get on all fours with your hands under your shoulders and your knees under your hips. Bring your buttocks back toward your heels, pulling your navel in against your spine as you do so. Rest your abdomen on your thighs and your head on the floor.

2 Take your arms back so that your hands are close to your feet. Hold the pose for a count of 15, then relax.

TWO-WEEK PLAN

Here is a simple two-week plan for you to follow. Although these exercises are grouped into 6-minute sessions, if you are new to exercise, don't feel you have to start out by doing the whole routine—you can build up the amount of time you spend and the types of exercises you do. You can also make up your own routines. The exercises in this book will tone your stomach muscles quickly, but be aware that they are not for fitness or weight loss.

Do what feels right for you

This exercise plan suggests you do one routine every day. However, if you do not usually exercise regularly, start by doing the routines every other day. Each routine should take about 6 minutes, depending on the number of reps. The workouts build in intensity, so repeat the first week's routine until you feel ready to incorporate the second week's more challenging schedule into your two-week program.

Making the most of your workout
• Always warm up before you begin.
• Think about what you are trying to achieve and be aware of how your body feels as you move.
• Remember to tighten your abdominal muscles.
• Keep your spine in neutral.
• Breathe in to prepare and breathe out as you move into position.
• Move slowly and gracefully.
• Cool down at the end to relax and bring your body back to normal.

Day 1
Roll down the wall: *5 reps* **p. 16**
Standing leg lift: *4-6 reps* **p. 18**
Basic squat: *6-8 reps* **p. 20**
Sitting forward spine stretch: *4 reps* **p. 21**
Sitting spinal twist: *8-10 reps on each side* **p. 21**
Sitting pelvic tilt: *10-15 reps* **p. 23**

Day 2
Rolling like a ball: *3-5 reps* **p. 27**
Reverse curl: *6-8 reps* **p. 29**
Oblique curl: *6-8 reps on each side* **p. 29**
Basic bridge: *2 reps* **p. 30**
Supine leg lift: *6-8 reps* **p. 35**
Side leg circles: *6-8 reps on each side* **p. 41**

Day 3

Standing forward bend: *5 reps* **p. 16**

Standing leg lift: *4-6 reps* **p. 18**

Lunge: *6-8 reps on each side* **p. 19**

Sitting leg lift: *3-5 reps on each leg* **p. 22**

Mermaid: *3 reps on each side* **p. 23**

Sitting reverse abdominal
curl: *6-8 reps* **p. 24**

Day 4

Dog: *4 reps* **p. 27**

Basic curl on an exercise
ball: *6-8 reps* **p. 28**

Swan: *2 reps* **p. 34**

Easy plank: *3 reps* **p. 33**

Prone leg raise: *6-8 reps on each leg* **p. 36**

Side leg circles: *6-8 reps on each side* **p. 41**

Day 6

Backstroke: *6-8 reps with each arm* **p. 26**

Reverse curl: *6-8 reps* **p. 29**

Oblique curl: *6-8 reps on each side* **p. 29**

Reverse bridge on an exercise ball: *2 reps* **p. 32**

Supine back extension: *2 reps* **p. 37**

Single-leg stretch: *6-8 reps* **p. 39**

Day 5

Horizontal balance: *1 rep on each leg* **p. 17**

Side standing leg lift: *6-8 reps
on each side* **p. 19**

Lunge: *6-8 reps on each
side* **p. 19**

Squat with leg lift: *6-8 reps
on each side* **p. 20**

Sitting spinal twist: *8-10 reps
reps on each side* **p. 21**

Sitting reverse abdominal
curl: *6-8 reps* **p. 24**

Day 7

Standing forward
bend: *5 reps* **p. 16**

Standing leg lift:
4-6 reps **p. 18**

Lunge: *6-8 reps on each side* **p. 19**

Sitting leg lift: *3-5 reps on each leg* **p. 22**

Sitting spinal twist: *8-10 reps
on each side* **p. 21**

Sitting reverse abdominal curl:
6-8 reps **p. 24**

Day 9

Roll down the wall: *5 reps* **p. 16**

Standing leg lift variation: *4-6 reps on each leg* **p. 18**

Squat with leg lift: *6-8 reps on each side* **p. 20**

Sitting leg lift: *6-8 reps both legs at once* **p. 22**

Mermaid: *6 reps on each side* **p. 23**

Sitting lateral curl: *6-8 reps on each side* **p. 25**

Day 8

Rolling like a ball: *3-5 reps* **p. 27**

Basic bridge variation: *2 reps* **p. 30**

Bridge with leg extension: *6-8 reps on each side* **p. 31**

Double-leg stretch: *6-8 reps* **p. 40**

Supine leg lift: *6-8 reps* **p. 35**

Scissors: *6-8 reps* **p. 36**

Day 10

Dog: *4 reps* **p. 27**

Plank: *3 reps* **p. 33**

Swan: *2 reps* **p. 34**

Prone leg raise: *6-8 reps on each leg* **p. 36**

Superman: *6-8 reps on each leg* **p. 38**

Side leg circles: *6-8 reps on each side* **p. 41**

TWO-WEEK PLAN

Day 11

Standing leg lift: *4-6 reps* **p. 18**

Basic squat: *6-8 reps* **p. 20**

Sitting forward spine stretch: *4 reps* **p. 21**

Sitting spinal twist: *8-10 reps on each side* **p. 21**

Sitting pelvic tilt: *10-15 reps* **p. 23**

Sitting lateral curl: *6-8 reps on each side* **p. 25**

Day 12

Rolling like a ball: *3-5 reps* **p. 27**

Basic curl on an exercise ball: *6-8 reps*
p. 28

Basic bridge variation: *2 reps* **p. 30**

Bridge with leg extension: *6-8 reps*
on each side **p. 31**

Scissors: *6-8 reps* **p. 36**

Side leg circles: *6-8 reps on each side* **p. 41**

Day 13

Horizontal balance: *1 rep on each leg* **p. 17**

Side standing leg lift: *6-8 reps on each side*
p. 19

Squat with leg lift: *6-8 reps on each side* **p. 20**

Sitting leg lift: *6-8 reps both legs*
at once **p. 22**

Mermaid: *6 reps on each side* **p. 23**

Sitting lateral curl: *6-8 reps*
on each side **p. 25**

Day 14

Basic curl on an exercise ball: *6-8 reps* **p. 28**

Reverse bridge on an exercise ball: *2 reps* **p. 32**

Push-up on a wobble board: *6-8 reps* **p. 33**

Swan on an exercise ball: *3 reps* **p. 34**

Superman variation: *2 reps* **p. 38**

Double-leg stretch: *6-8 reps* **p. 40**

INDEX